Light

Claire Llewellyn

Photography by Ray Moller

W

FRANKLIN WATTS
LONDON • SYDNEY

First published 2003 by Franklin Watts
96 Leonard Street, London EC2A 4XD

Franklin Watts Australia
45-51 Huntley Street
Alexandria, NSW 2015

Text copyright © Claire Llewellyn 2003
Design and concept © Franklin Watts 2003

Series advisor: Gill Matthews, non-fiction literacy
consultant and Inset trainer
Editor: Rachel Cooke
Series design: Peter Scoulding
Designer: James Marks
Photography: Ray Moller unless otherwise credited
Acknowledgements: Automobile Association: 21t, 23cr. Vicki Coombs/Ecoscene: 7.
Jeri Gleiters/Still Pictures: 12. Tim Hawkins/Eye Ubiquitous: 5. Michael Heller/911 Pictures: 20.
Frank Leather/Eye Ubiquitous: 11b. Helen A. Lisher/Eye Ubiquitous: 16. Stephen Rafferty/Eye
Ubiquitous: 6. John A Read/Eye Ubiquitous: 11t. Norbert Schafer/Corbis: 4, 22l. Craig
Tuttle/Corbis: 21b. Thanks to our models: Chloe Chetty, Georgia Farrell, Arden Farrow, Alex
Green, Madison Hanley, Aaron Hibbert, Chetan Johal, James Moller, Henry Moller, Kane Yoon.

A CIP catalogue record for this book is available from the British Library

ISBN: 0 7496 5167 9

Printed in Malaysia

Contents

Daylight

In the morning, the Sun rises.
It gives us light during the day.

▶ *In daylight,
we can see
the world
around us.*

Cloudy days are duller than sunny days because clouds block some of the light.

Night-time

In the evening, the Sun sets and the sky gets dark. We need other lights to help us see.

▶ *Car drivers put on their lights.*

▲ *Streetlights come on.*

At night, rooms are dark without the lights on. How can you make your bedroom dark during the day?

People put on lights in their houses.

Electric light

We use electricity to light
our homes.

▲ *Electric light helps us to see –*
in the living room...

▲ *in the bedroom…*

Torches give out light. They get electricity from batteries so we can carry torches around.

◀ *and in the fridge!*

Firelight

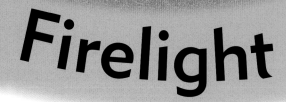

Fire gives out light, too.
A small fire gives
just a little light.
A big one gives
much more!

▼ *Candles*

Firelight is pretty but it is dangerous. Never play with fire.

A bonfire

Fireworks!

Shadow play

Some things block out light.
This can make shadows.

▲ *Trees block the Sun's light.*
They make shadows on the ground.

Our hand blocks the torch's light. It makes a shadow.

Stick some white paper on a wall and shine a bright light on it. Sit sideways between the light and paper so your head makes a shadow on the paper. Ask a friend to draw round your shadow.

Seeing

We see with our eyes.
Our eyes need light to see.

▶ *We see when light enters our eyes.*

How can you find your way around when your eyes are closed?

▶ *If we cover our eyes, light cannot enter them and we cannot see.*

15

Bright and shiny

Shiny things reflect the light.
Light makes them stand out brightly.

▲ *Glass balls shine in the dark.*

What other things can you think of that are bright and shiny?

▲ *A ring is bright and shiny.*

▶ *Sweet wrappers are bright and shiny too!*

Be safe, be seen!

Wearing things that reflect light helps to keep us safe at night. People can see us more clearly.

▶ *This bag reflects the lights of a car.*

◄ *This coat reflects light.*

How can you make sure you are easy to spot at night?

◄ *This cyclist wears a shiny strap.*

Danger!

Bright lights are easy to see.
They help to warn people of danger.

Danger!

▲ *... a police car is coming!*

Many warning lights flash on and off. Can you think why?

▲ ... a car has broken down!

◀ ... there are rocks nearby!

I know that...

1 The Sun gives us light during the day.

2 We must never look directly at the Sun.

3 It is dark at night because there is no sunlight.

4 We use electric lights in our homes.

5 Fire gives out light, too.

6 Shadows form when something blocks out light.

7 We see when light enters our eyes.

8 Shiny things reflect light.

9 Lights can warn us of danger.

Index

About this book

I Know That! is designed to introduce children to the process of gathering information and using reference books, one of the key skills needed to begin more formal learning at school. For this reason, each book's structure reflects the information books children will use later in their learning career – with key information in the main text and additional facts and ideas in the captions. The panels give an opportunity for further activities, ideas or discussions. The contents page and index are helpful reference guides.

The language is carefully chosen to be accessible to children just beginning to read. Illustrations support the text but also give information in their own right; active consideration and discussion of images is another key referencing skill. The main aim of the series is to build confidence – showing children how much they already know and giving them the ability to gather new information for themselves. With this in mind, the *I know that...* section at the end of the book is a simple way for children to revisit what they already know as well as what they have learnt from reading the book.